PAKISTAN

A **TRUE BOOK**®

by
Ann Heinrichs

Children's Press®
A Division of Scholastic Inc.

New York Toronto London Auckland Sydney
Mexico City New Delhi Hong Kong
Danbury, Connecticut

A Pakistani rides in a colorfully painted truck.

Reading Consultant
Sonja I. Smith
Reading Specialist

Content Consultant
Dr. Amy J. Johnson, Ph.D.
Berry College

Library of Congress Cataloging-in-Publication Data

Heinrichs, Ann.
　　Pakistan / Ann Heinrichs.
　　　　p. cm. — (A true book)
Includes bibliographical references and index.
Contents: Mountains, valleys, and deserts—The human landscape—
Becoming a nation—Pakistanis at work—Customs and daily life.
　　ISBN 0-516-22813-7 (lib. bdg.)　　0-516-26962-3 (pbk.)
　　1. Pakistan—Juvenile literature. [1. Pakistan.] I. Title. II. Series.
DS376.9.H452 2004
954.91—dc22

　　　　　　　　　　　　　　　　　　　　　　　　　　　　2003018662

Contents

Mountains, Valleys, and Deserts 5

The Human Landscape 14

Cultures and Empires 22

An Independent Nation 28

Daily Life in Pakistan 34

To Find Out More 44

Important Words 46

Index 47

Meet the Author 48

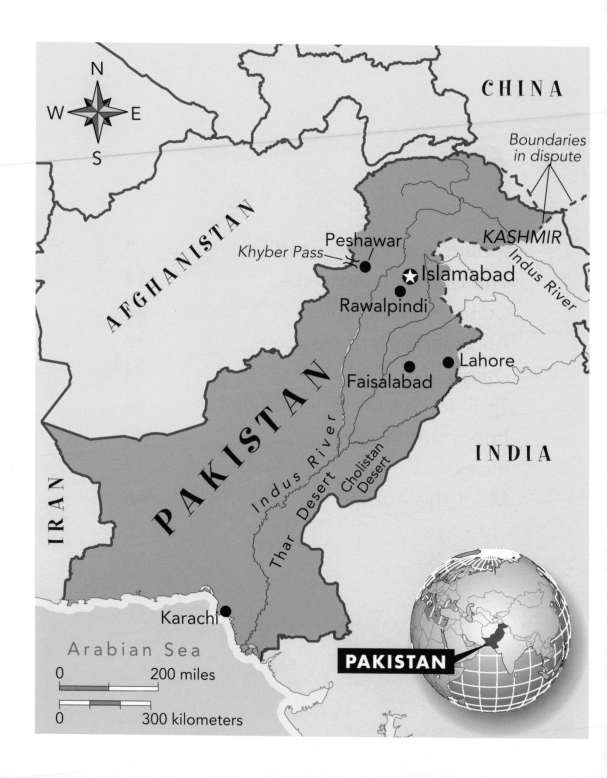

Mountains, Valleys, and Deserts

Pakistan is a land of snowy mountains, green valleys, and arid deserts. It is located in south Asia, on a landmass called the Indian **subcontinent**. Pakistan, India, and several smaller countries occupy this huge, diamond-shaped region.

Pakistan shares its eastern border with India. To the north and west is Afghanistan. China lies to the northeast, and Iran borders the southwest. On the south, Pakistan faces the Arabian Sea, which is part of the Indian Ocean.

Northeastern Pakistan contains the Jammu and Kashmir region. It is often called simply Kashmir. Both Pakistan and India govern parts of this area.

Jagged, snow-capped peaks cover northern Pakistan. They

Hikers explore the glacial ice and high peaks of the Karakoram Mountains.

belong to the Himalaya, Karakoram, and Hindu Kush mountain ranges. Among these mountains are some of the world's highest peaks. Huge glaciers, or masses of ice, stand

A camel stops to rest in the Thar Desert.

among the mountains. Sparkling lakes and **fertile** valleys nestle beneath the towering peaks.

The dry, rocky Baluchistan Plateau covers southwestern Pakistan. In the southeast are

the Thar and Cholistan deserts.
The Cholistan's sand dunes
shift in the dry desert winds.

The Indus River runs through
Pakistan from north to south. It
rushes down from the northern

The Indus River

mountains and winds across broad plains. At last it empties into the Arabian Sea. Several rivers flow into the Indus, making the Indus River Valley a fertile farming region. Karachi,

Pakistan's largest city, lies near the mouth of the Indus River.

Bears, deer, wild sheep, and mountain goats roam Pakistan's mountains. Snow leopards live there, too. They have become rare because of overhunting.

Snow leopards live in the mountains of Central Asia. Their coloring helps keep them hidden on the rocky slopes.

Herds of antelope graze across the plains.

Forests cover the lower mountainsides, but these

Sawmill workers in Hunza turn trees into lumber.

forests are quickly thinning out. Many people cut down the trees for firewood. Others clear them to make room for farms or factories.

From April through June, Pakistan is hot and dry. Monsoons, or heavy rains, sweep through the region from July to September. Winter lasts from December through March, when the weather turns cool. In the mountains, winter can be bitterly cold.

The Human Landscape

More than 153 million people live in Pakistan. The country is divided into four provinces—Punjab, Sind, Baluchistan, and the North-West Frontier.

People of many ethnic groups live in Pakistan. Punjabis make up more than half the population. Their traditional

A Punjabi man

homeland is the Punjab province. The Sindhi are mainly in Sind province in the south. Many Sindhi are farmers. Pashtuns live in the North-West Frontier province and also occupy **tribal**

A Baluchi girl

areas along the western
border. Baluchi people live in
Baluchistan, in the southwest.
They are **nomads**, moving with
their herds of sheep and goats
from place to place. Other
peoples in Pakistan include the

Saraiki, Hindko, and Brahui. Also, many tribal **ethnic** groups live in the high mountains.

Urdu is Pakistan's official language. However, each of Pakistan's ethnic groups has its own language. The major languages are Punjabi, Sindhi,

In some parts of Pakistan, signs are written in more than one language.

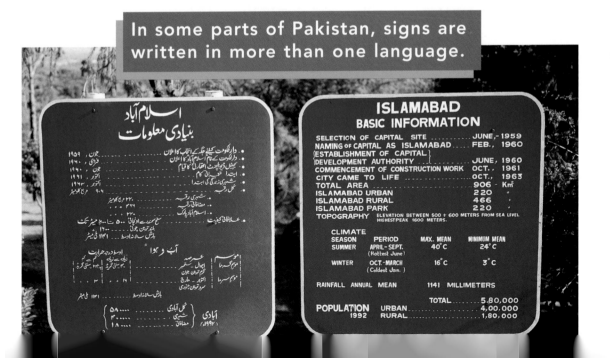

Baluchi, and Pashtu. English is also often used by government officials and businesses.

Islam is Pakistan's official religion. About 97 of every 100 Pakistanis are Muslims, or followers of Islam. Muslims believe in the same God worshipped by Christian and Jewish people. Muslims call God by the name Allah. They honor Muhammad, the founder of Islam, as Allah's messenger. Their holy scripture is the

Young Muslims study the Qur'an.

Qur'an, or Koran. Small communities of Christians and Hindus also live in Pakistan.

Religion is an important part of daily life. Five times a day,

Muslims kneel and bow in prayer. Friday is a holy day, when schools and shops close and people attend services in a **mosque.** Many beautiful mosques are located through-out the country.

Islamic Holidays

In celebration of Eid al-Fitr, some Pakistans decorate their skin with henna, a reddish-brown dye.

Religious holidays are important events in Pakistan. The feast of Eid al-Adha celebrates the prophet Abraham's willingness to sacrifice his son to God. Another big feast is Eid al-Fitr. It celebrates the end of Ramadan, the Islamic month of fasting. Both holidays are celebrated with special prayers and hearty feasts eaten with family and friends.

Cultures and Empires

Pakistan became a nation of its own in 1947. Before that, Pakistan and India were one nation. Because they shared the Indian subcontinent, they also shared many of the same rulers, beliefs, and ways of life.

Around 2500 B.C., a great **culture** grew up in the Indus River Valley.

The remains of Mohenjo Daro, an ancient city built on the banks of the Indus River

Its people had well-developed writing, trade, and government systems. Homes with courtyards stood along the wide city streets.

Around 1500 B.C., Aryan people spread into the subcontinent from present-day Iran. Their religion was the basis of today's Hindu faith.

Many empires ruled Pakistan in the next centuries. In the 500s B.C., the Persian Empire spread into Pakistan from Iran. Greek armies invaded in the 300s B.C. Next, Pakistan was ruled by the Mauryan Empire, centered in present-day India. The Kushan Empire of the A.D. 100s ruled from western Pakistan.

In the 700s, people from Saudi Arabia arrived with their religion of Islam. In time, most of Pakistan embraced Islam. In 1526, a Muslim prince named Bābur

A painting of Bābur (right center), founder of the Mughal Empire

invaded from central Asia. His Mughal Empire stretched across present-day India and Pakistan. Pakistan's arts and literature, or written works, flourished under the Mughals.

British officials in India in the 1820s

Soon European traders arrived. By the 1800s, the British not only controlled the region's trade, but also conquered and ruled the subcontinent. Movements for freedom from Britain began to sweep through the land.

The Father of Pakistan

Muhammad Ali Jinnah (1876–1948) is known as the Father of Pakistan. Jinnah was a lawyer from Karachi who became president of the All-India Muslim League. This was an organization of Muslims in India. Jinnah pushed for a separate Muslim state, which would become known as Pakistan. He served as Pakistan's first governor-general from 1947 to 1948.

In Pakistan, Muhammad Ali Jinnah is known as "the Great Leader."

An Independent Nation

Independence came at last in 1947. The subcontinent was divided into two nations— Pakistan and India. The new Pakistan consisted of East and West Pakistan. East Pakistan became the separate nation of Bangladesh in 1971.

Since gaining independence, Pakistan has had periods of both **democratic** and military rule. Under democratic rule, the president is the head of state. He or she represents Pakistan in dealing with other countries. The parliament, with two houses, is the lawmaking body. One of those houses elects a prime minister. This official oversees day-to-day governing activities.

Pakistan has faced many challenges over the years. Several times it clashed with India over who would rule the Kashmir region. In the 1990s, people in neighboring Afghanistan suffered under a harsh government. Many Afghans fled to Pakistan. It was

hard for Pakistan to feed and
shelter them all. International
organizations came in to help.

A military officer, General
Pervez Musharraf, seized
power in 1999. He believed

the country's leaders were doing a poor job. As president, Musharraf has said that he will move the government back toward a democratic system.

In the early 2000s, **terrorists** carried out many bombings and killings in Pakistan. They wanted the country to have a strict government that allowed few freedoms. They also opposed Pakistan's ties with the United States. Pakistani officials worked hard to arrest

In 2002, a group of Christians in Pakistan protested recent terrorist attacks.

NO RELIGION Permits Terrorism

these terrorists and to keep
peace in the country.

Daily Life in Pakistan

Pakistanis are warm and friendly people. They welcome guests by serving them *chai,* a strong, spicy tea. Guests are often invited to stay for a meal.

Meals consist of fresh, locally grown foods. Chicken, lamb, and goat meat are mixed with fresh vegetables. Spicy sauces

A Pakistani family eats lunch together (above); Naan bread (right)

often add to the flavor. The typical bread is a round, flat loaf called *naan*. Alcohol and pork are forbidden by Islamic law.

Pakistanis dress modestly. Both men and women wear the *shalwar qamiz*. It consists of baggy pants and a long, loose shirt. Most women also cover their heads with a scarf or shawl. People of tribal ethnic groups wear traditional, colorful clothing.

Many Pakistanis live by farming and herding. Farmers on the central plains grow wheat, rice, sugarcane, and cotton. Factories make the

A shepherd moves his sheep through the Swat Valley.

A man works at a furniture factory in Peshawar.

cotton into thread, cloth, and finished clothes. Some farmers grow fruits, such as apples, apricots, peaches, and grapes. In the high mountains, herders tend flocks of sheep and goats.

Many people work in small craft shops or at home. They make handcrafted pottery, wood, and leather goods. Pakistan's handmade carpets are prized around the world.

Workers sort through colorful cotton fabrics made in Pakistan.

A village
in Punjab

Most Pakistanis live outside cities and towns. In small villages, people travel by foot or on donkeys. Homes are built of mud, clay, or bricks dried in the sun. Inside are two or three rooms with woven mats on the floors. People eat, meet guests, and sleep on the mats.

Cities are packed with cars, trucks, buses, and motorcycles. They share the streets with

Outdoor markets in Peshawar

donkey carts and chickens. Karachi and other big cities are overcrowded. Poor people live in tiny shacks along narrow streets. Those who are better off live in apartment buildings or beautiful homes.

Pakistanis value poetry, and people recite long poems for entertainment. In many regions, people perform colorful folk dances. These are joyful ways to celebrate culture in this diverse land.

Pakistanis performing a
traditional folk dance

To Find Out More

Here are some additional resources to help you learn more about Pakistan:

 **Books**

Demi. **Muhammad.** Margaret K. McElderry, 2003.

Ganeri, Anita. **The Qur'an and Islam.** Smart Apple Media, 2004.

Haque, Jameel. **Pakistan.** Gareth Stevens, 2002.

Hoyt-Goldsmith, Diane. **Celebrating Ramadan.** Holiday House, 2002.

Organizations and Online Sites

Embassy of the Islamic Republic of Pakistan
3517 International Court, NW
Washington, DC 20008
202-243-6500
*http://www.embassyof
pakistan.org*

Islamic Republic of Pakistan
http://www.infopak.gov.pk/

To learn about Pakistan's culture, history, and interesting places.

An Introduction to Pakistan
*http://www.interknowledge.
com/pakistan/index.html*

To explore Pakistan's history and geography, including famous mountains and valleys.

World Wildlife Federation: Pakistan
http://www.wwfpak.org

For fascinating information about Pakistan's animals, plants, and protected areas.

Important Words

culture the customs and ways of life of a group of people

democratic a form of government in which people elect their leaders

ethnic relating to a person's race or nationality

fertile able to produce many fruits or vegetables

mosque a place of worship for followers of the Islamic faith

nomads people who move from place to place as the seasons and food supplies change

subcontinent a large division of a continent

terrorists people who use fear and violence to force their will on others

tribal relating to close-knit groups of people who share the same race, customs, and ways of life

Index

(**Boldface** page numbers
indicate illustrations.)

All-India Muslim League, 27
ancient culture/civilizations,
    22–25
Bābur, 24–25, **25**
Baluchistan Plateau, 8
British rule, 26
camel, **8**
Cholistan Desert, 9
Christian protesters, **33**
cities, **41,** 41–42
climate, 13
clothing, 36–37
empires, 24–26
farms & farming, 10, **10,**
    37–38
folk dance, 42, **43**
food & meals, 34–35, **35**
forests, 12–13
geography, 6–13
government, 29–33
henna tattoos, 21, **21**
holidays, 21
housing & homes, 40–41, 42
independence, 28
Indus River & Valley, **9,**
    9–11, **10**

Islam, 18–21
Karachi, 10–11
languages, 17–18
lifestyle, 34–42
livestock, **37,** 38
Mohenjo Daro, **23**
mountains, 6–8, **7,** 11
Muhammad Ali Jinnah, 27,
    27
Musharraf, Pervez, 31, **31**
Muslim boys studying the
    Qur'an, **19**
Muslims kneel in prayer, **20**
nomads, 16
Parliament House, **29**
people, 14–17, **15, 16**
poetry, 42
population, 14
Punjab village, **40**
religion, 18–21
sawmill workers, **12**
sheep, **37**
snow leopards, 11, **11**
terrorism, 32–33
Thar Desert, **8,** 8–9
wildlife, **11,** 11–12
working & employment,
    37–39

Meet the Author

Ann Heinrichs grew up in Arkansas and lives in Chicago, Illinois. She has written more than one hundred books about American, European, Asian, and African history and culture. Several of her books have won national and regional awards.

Besides the United States, she has traveled in Europe, Africa, the Middle East, and East Asia. The desert is her favorite terrain.

Ms. Heinrichs holds bachelor's and master's degrees in piano performance. She practices tai chi empty-hand and sword forms and has won many awards in martial arts competitions.